THE OXEN
AND THE
SPIDERS

HOW TEAMWORK BUILDS
AN UNUSUAL FRIENDSHIP

To: Daisy Belanger

**Story and Illustrations by
Kathy Salanitro**

Moos:chip, Jake, Max & Dale

Kathy Salanitro

The events that take place in this book are fiction. The characters are real. The oxen and the spiders live in a barn in Gilford, New Hampshire. The ceiling of that barn has spider webs that do get covered in the dust from the oxen jumping around. The spiders repeatedly abandon these webs and form new ones to continue catching flies.

Book design by Robin Wrighton
robin@robinwrighton.com

First Edition
ISBN: 978-0-9966621-0-9

Published by
Ox-K Farm
Gilford, New Hampshire
www.oxkfarm.com

For information on special purchases contact: oxkfarmbooks@gmail.com

Printed in Lowell, Massachusetts by King Printing Company

DEDICATION

I dedicate this book to all who helped and encouraged me
through the whole process of writing my first book.

To my husband Ron Salanitro, family and friends,
who were my sounding board and believed in and encouraged me.

To MaryBeth Godbout, without her commitment to education,
this book would never have gotten started.

Guided encouragement was gratefully received from the following:

Abi Maxwell, an author in her own right.
Anita Craven, Melissa Johnson, Lisa Carlson, Robert Pelkie.

Special thanks go to the following people:

Peter Szawlowski, who photographed my paintings.
Jean Cox, from Art Escape in Laconia NH, for guidance during the painting.
Robin Wrighton, whose expertise helped assemble this beautiful book.
Tony Lancia, from Running Brook Art Gallery, for the portrait of Chip and Kathy.

hip, Dale, Jake and Max, four ox brothers, are lying down in the barn out of the hot summer sun for an afternoon nap. Feeling something falling on his head, Max wakes from his nap. He looks up at the ceiling and sees something move as dirt falls into his eyes.

"Hey! Who are you and what are you doing?" he moos loudly.

"Oh hi, my name is Yellow." A spider drops down on a single strand of web and lands on Max's nose and replies, "I'm cleaning your dirt off my web."

Max blinks to refocus and sees on the end of his nose a big yellow spider with black stripes. He moos, "It's my barn!"

Dale, blinking his eyes from the fallen dirt, hears Max yell. Turning to look, he sees the spider on Max's nose. "What's going on?" Dale moos.

Max replies, "This is Yellow, a spider that is dropping dirt from his web onto my fur and into my eyes."

Dale glares at Yellow and demands, "Yellow, why are you throwing dirt at us?"

"We are cleaning your dirt off our webs." Yellow responds.

Dale asks, "Who are 'we'?"

"Me and my friends," says Yellow, as he crawls back up the strand to his web. "Let me introduce them to you. To my left is Brownie. She is a barn spider and makes big webs to catch flies,"

Brownie waves with one of her eight legs.

"This is Stretch on the right," Yellow says. "He is a daddy long legs. Stretch makes cobwebs to catch bugs."

"Hi," Stretch says, waving one of his long front legs.

"This is Hoppy on Stretch's right. He is a jumping spider that can hop from post to post to catch bugs," continues Yellow.

Waving his front leg in greeting, Hoppy blurts out, "Hi! Watch me hop from the barn ceiling to that post and back to the ceiling in a blink of an eye. I don't make webs like Yellow and the others, but look at the lifeline I make when I jump so I don't fall."

Dale moos up at all the spiders, "Why are you here in our barn?"

Yellow sighs in frustration. "Well, my three spider friends and I have been looking for a home. We saw you four oxen in this large, nice, warm barn and thought there'd be plenty of room for all of us. You live down there on the ground and we live up here on the ceiling. You'll barely notice we are here. We will help you out by building webs and eating the flies that come in and bite you."

Glaring at Yellow, Max shakes the cobwebs and dirt off his horns and fur and says, "Yellow! You are getting dirt all over me and I don't like it. We didn't ask you to move in here and eat flies."

"Hi Yellow, I'm Chip and I don't like flies biting me. Thank you for eating them."

Looking at his ox brothers, Chip moos matter-of-factly, "I don't have any dirt falling on me."

"Chip," Max cries, "that's because they are not building their webs over you!"

Jake pipes up with a moo, "Dale and Max, I agree with Chip. I don't like flies either, but I just shake off the little dirt that falls on me." Jake stands and shakes himself vigorously. "See! Now you can't see it."

Impatient with anger, Max stands up and stomps his hoof, "Jake, go right ahead and agree with Chip. They're not building webs over him."

"Calm down Max, I think the spiders can help us out," moos Jake.

Max looks over at Dale. "Say something Dale. You're in charge of the barn and I don't want those spiders over us. I want them to leave."

Standing up, Dale says, "Chip and Jake, I agree with Max. I think the spiders have to go."

With the decision made, the four oxen glare intently up at the four spiders.

"Yellow," Dale says sternly, "my brothers and I have decided that you spiders must leave our barn now."

Upset by what they have been told, Yellow yells down to the four oxen, "It's not our fault that our webs are dirty. You four come in here and jump around in the sawdust, lock horns and kick up all the dust. That dust gets all over our webs and the flies won't stick. If you kept a cleaner barn, that wouldn't happen!"

The four ox brothers yell all together, "OUT OF OUR BARN!"

With no argument left to be made, Yellow, Brownie, Stretch and Hoppy pack up their webs into their little suitcases and leave the barn. Looking at each other, they wonder where to go.

Brownie sobs, "I only like to live in barns. Where are we going to live now?"

Hoppy, bouncing in circles around Yellow adds, "Winter will come and it's going to get cold."

"You both make good points," says Yellow sadly.

Moving on long legs, Stretch walks far ahead of the other spiders.

"Hey Stretch!" Yellow hollers. "Slow up and wait for us. We can find a new home if we just stay together," Yellow suggests.

The three spiders look at Yellow and agree.

Hoppy jumps up and down, pointing and yelling. "Look! Look at those trees. Look at all the flies and bugs flying around them. Let's live there."

Yellow stops and thinks, this IS a good place. The trees along the riverbank are tall to keep us dry and the water will bring us more bugs.

The four spiders quickly agree to set up their new web homes in the trees. Yellow and Stretch choose to live on the east side of the river. Brownie and Hoppy decide to go over the bridge and live on the west side.

The next morning, farmer Kathy enters the barn to feed the oxen. Chip, Dale, Jake and Max came to live with Kathy when they were just week-old bull calves and weighed only 60 pounds. Over time, Kathy taught them how to work together as a team in a yoke. They all love Kathy and give her hugs by wrapping their necks around her and placing big licks on her arm or cheek. She gives them motherly kisses on the top of their heads and calls them her boys. Even though they are now four-year-old grown up oxen and weigh 2,500 pounds each, they still have to listen to Kathy, whom they consider mom.

Finishing their breakfast, Dale asks, "Mom, can we go down to the river and take a swim?"

"OK," replies Kathy. "You can go, but don't go into the deep water. The river is running fast and it could pull you downstream."

"OK! We will be careful," the four oxen say in unison.

First outside of the barn, Dale yells back to his brothers, "I'll race you to the river."

Hooves pound the ground as the four oxen take off. What a sight they make! Running as fast as they can with their tails straight out, eyes squinting and wind brushing back their fur.

Reaching the riverbank first, Dale shouts, "Here I go!"

Leaping forward with a giant SPLASH, Dale jumps into the water. Max and Jake, with huge splashes of their own, follow their brother into the river. Chip, on the other hand, stops, looks both ways, and calmly walks into the water. Dipping his horns low into the water, he splashes with delight.

Slap, slap, slap! All the horns hit the water as hard as they can. Hearing all their noise, Kathy walks down the path to the river to check on her boys.

"Boys! Are you being careful?" Kathy calls out.

Hearing Kathy's call, four sets of horns, rise up from the river. Then there are four sets of eyes. Finally, four long noses with water dripping off the ends appear.

"We are, we are," they gleefully moo back to Kathy.

Knowing her boys are having fun, Kathy turns back up the path to return to the garden.

"Max, what are you doing?" calls out Chip.

"I'm swimming, Chip. What do you think I am doing?"

"Max, Mom said not to go into the deep water."

"Oh Chip, you are such a worry wart. I am a grown up ox now, I can do what I want."

Turning his back on Max in the deeper water, Chip heads back upstream to play with Jake and Dale. Still, Chip has a bad feeling about Max.

All of a sudden Max starts bellowing and loudly moos, "Help! Help!"

The three brothers quickly turn to look back towards the yelling.

Frantically bobbing up and down in the deep water, Max resurfaces again and yells louder, "Help me! I can't touch the bottom and the water is pulling me under. HELP!"

Dale and Chip start to swim out to help Max.

Jake yells, "Wait! Don't go too far. We will get caught in the deep water too. I have a plan. Dale I will hold your tail in my mouth and stand here on the edge of the riverbank. You swim out a little way and grab Chip's tail in your mouth. Then Chip will swim out farther and reach for Max's tail. Once Chip has Max's tail in his mouth, we can slowly walk backwards and pull Max to the riverbank."

Forming the lifeline, Chip swims to Max calling, "Max, reach out your tail so I can grab it."

Max raises his tail out of the water and Chip grabs it with his mouth. Jake and Dale begin backing up to the riverbank. It is slow-going. The swift-moving water is pulling hard on Max. The three brothers continue straining and pulling with all their might. Jake, with his back legs bent a little under him, is anchoring the oxen-made lifeline. Holding a mouthful of Chip's tail, Dale slips a little in the soft mud. Digging his hooves deeper into the river bottom, he feels a reassuring tug on his tail by Jake. Farther out into the water, Chip's weight is on his back hooves, but his front legs are swinging in the rushing water as he holds tightly onto Max's tail. Chip thinks, if I can only get my front hooves to touch the mud under the water, I can pull Max better.

"Pull! Pull! I can't touch bottom yet," Max yells.

Suddenly, Chip hears little snapping sounds as pieces of Max's tail start to break. SPLASH! The three oxen fall back into the water. They hastily jump up.

"What happened, Dale?"

"I don't know, Jake."

They look at Chip with a mouth full of Max's tail hair.

"Help! Help! I'm going down the river again. Help!" moos Max.

Watching Max being pulled farther and farther down the river, the three brothers get the feeling they may lose their brother. In despair, they look at each other. They've tried so very hard, but now they're out of ideas.

Chip takes off in a full run.

"Where are you going Chip," Dale yells.

"I'm going to get Mom." Chip yells over his shoulder.

Hearing the thundering hooves, Kathy rushes out to meet Chip at the break in the tree line.

"What happened?" Kathy asks.

"Max is in deep water and can't get out. He's floating too far down the river and we don't know what to do," Chip breathlessly tells Kathy.

The two quickly run down the path to the river.

Meeting up with the other brothers, they all start running along the riverbank. They watch helplessly as Max's head bobs in and out of the water. Crying in despair, they fear Max is going to drown.

Max tries desperately to keep his nose above the water so he can breathe, but the hard work is wearing him out and the water is getting deeper around him. All that is visible to Kathy and his brothers is Max's nose and the tips of his horns. The rest of his body is under the swirling river water. Kathy and Dale, Chip and Jake huddle together to comfort each other as their weeping grows louder.

Dale spies urgent movement in the trees above them. He yells, "Mom, look in the trees. It's the spiders from the barn. What are they doing?"

"I don't know Dale," answers Kathy.

They all look up with intense interest and watch the spiders hastily race to the end of the branches and look down at Max.

"Look," moos Dale, "the yellow spider seems to be signaling to the two spiders across the river."

Kathy and the ox brothers look on in amazement. They watch as Yellow jumps from the tree with a web attached down to Max's horn. He quickly attaches his sticky web to Max's horn and with his entire spider strength pulls one side of Max's head up out of the water.

Yellow realizes Max is too enormous and he cannot hold on all by himself. Yellow shouts rapid orders to Stretch, Brownie and Hoppy.

Stretch jumps from his tree branch to Max's head with a web. He knits the web around Max's other horn. Yellow and Stretch tug together hoping their webs will hold. Max's ears and eyes appear above the water, but Yellow knows there is still much more to be done. The water is running fast and still splashing over Max's head.

Worn out and disorientated, Max starts to hear voices. He strains to hear what the voices are saying. In a few moments he realizes it's the spiders!

Carrying on with his orders, Yellow shouts, "Brownie tie a web from your tree to Max's head and side."

As Yellow and Brownie work, Hoppy firmly attaches a network of lifelines between Max's back and the trees.

Relieved, Max thinks, they are trying to help me. I have to calm down and hold still. I only need to swim a little with my legs to keep myself afloat. I am so tired. I still must try. A feeling of encouragement comes over Max as he is held in place by the curtain of webs. He realizes that the spiders have stopped him from floating farther down river, but he still has doubts. I am so enormous compared to their size. How are they going to save me? I will just have to trust they know what they are doing and remain calm.

Hundreds of webs extend from trees on both sides of the river down to where the spiders have skillfully attached them to Max's horns, back and tail. Kathy and the brothers' sobs begin to quiet as their despair turns to hope. They don't know what to think. Will this work? They stand silently and watch as the spiders intently spin their webs. As fast as they can, the spiders continue to cover Max in webs and he feels himself being raised higher and higher in the middle of the river.

Yellow shouts more orders. "Brownie and Hoppy, make your webs longer. Stretch and I will pull Max to his brothers on the riverbank."

Everyone watches breathlessly, as Max slowly floats sideways to the riverbank.

Once his feet touch the bottom in shallow water, Max yells, "My feet! My feet! I can touch the mud under the water."

Kathy and Max's brothers jump up and down and cheer as Max moves to the riverbank. Exhausted, he can hardly stand.

They rush over to Max. Kathy grabs his horns, while Chip and Dale tug his collar and Jake nudges him from behind.

Overjoyed to be back on dry land, Max collapses from exhaustion.

Satisfied that Max is now safe, the spiders cut their connecting webs and watch the happy reunion from the tree branches above. Though the spiders feel forgotten, they are proud they have done a good thing today.

Everyone is so happy to see Max safe. His brothers lick the webs off his back, while Kathy pulls the webs from his horns.

Sheepishly looking up at Kathy from where he lays on the ground, Max says, "Mom, I'm sorry. I thought I knew better and that I was big enough to swim in the river."

"Ok Max, don't worry about that now. Just relax so we can clean you off."

"Mom, the spiders saved me."

"I know Max, they did."

"Mom, where are they?"

Everyone looks up into the trees and sees the spiders sitting there on a branch looking down at them.

With gratitude in his voice, Max gently calls to the spiders, "Yellow, Stretch, Brownie, Hoppy, thank you!"

Kathy and the oxen cheer for the heroic spiders.

The next morning, Max wakes up thinking about what happened to him at the river. He knows without the help of the spiders and everyone working together, things could have turned out much worse.

Max tells his bothers, "You know, it was the spiders who saved my life yesterday. I think it would be a nice gesture to ask them to live with us here in our barn."

"Yes, yes," they all agree.

"But how are we going to keep them from dropping dirt on us? I still want to be able to play in the barn and jump around," Dale asks.

"All we have to do is help them keep their webs clean," answers Max.

The four oxen agree that if they all work together as a team, they and the spiders can live happily together.

The four brothers return to the river in search of the four spiders. Looking up, they see the spiders in the trees.

Max moos kindly up to the spiders, "Yellow, my brothers and I would like to thank you and your three friends for your help yesterday. We would like all of you to come back and live with us in the barn."

Grateful for the invitation, the spiders pack their little suitcases. Yellow, Stretch, Brownie and Hoppy excitedly swing down on their webs onto the back of each ox.

Arriving at the barn, the spiders and oxen look up and see the webs and ceiling are full of dust and dirt.

"Max, we can't live in those webs full of dirt. What are we going to do?" asks Yellow.

Looking up at the messy ceiling Max replies, "You are right Yellow."

Max calls out to his brothers, "Please bring me the duster, the stepstool and the dust mask. Let's clean this place up."

Stepping onto the stepstool and reaching up with a duster in his mouth and a dust mask over his nose, Max dusts down the cobwebs from the ceiling. Yellow points out where to clean, as Stretch, Brownie and Hoppy begin the task of making new webs.

To this day, if the light is just right on a warm sunny day, you may see a spider web spun between two oxen horns and a spider riding in the middle of the web.

FUN FACTS

What Are Oxen?

OXEN can be any breed of cattle

COW – Mother

BULL – Father

CALVES – Babies

HEIFER – Baby girl calf

BULL CALF – Baby boy calf

STEER – Altered bull calf at 6 to 9 months

WORKING STEER – Steer trained to work

OX – Four plus year old Working Steer

OX – One

OXEN – Two or more

Steers and oxen cannot become fathers

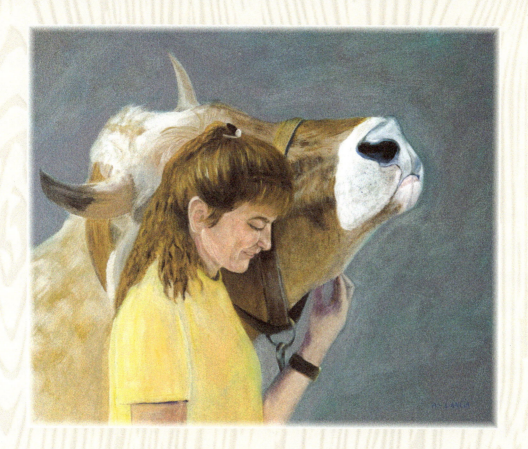

ABOUT THE AUTHOR

Kathy Salanitro and her husband built their house in 1981 in Gilford NH and started raising and training oxen. In 2004, Kathy trained the four oxen from this story (Chip, Dale, Jake and Max) as therapy oxen. In 2009, she started Ox-K Farm Discovery Center, which is dedicated to enriching children and young people's lives by guiding and encouraging them to develop self-discipline, patience and self-confidence through interaction with oxen. Kathy has worked with children of all ages and with many challenges. She has witnessed their growth of self-confidence while interacting with the oxen. In 2011, Kathy won the title and crown for Ms. NH Senior America, her platform and talent was making a difference in children's lives with oxen. While Kathy was in isolation recovering from cancer treatment, she decided to put the time to good use and write a story using oxen.